THE SURPRISING POWER OF

THE COIL

GREG CAMPBELL
AND DR. STEVE HALLIDAY

What others are saying about *The Coil*

"Everyone wins when we are open to connecting relationally with the people around us, even when we don't know what might come of it. The author's love of people and his leadership success at the highest levels of business make him the right person to write about this."

—**Mark Aardsma**, entrepreneur, investor, author

Greg Campbell's concise and inspiring book does what only the best business books do: compel the reader to act."

—**Scott Monday**, partner, Kitchen Crate

"I've found the insights in Greg Campbell's writing to be helpful in a number of areas of life, but "The Coil," the team term the author uses to describe the network of social connections we all have, is likely the most helpful in how I've thought about life, even outside of networking. These are principles that apply to all of life and I really enjoyed the book."

—**Jeffery M. Smith**, Facebook

"Greg's wisdom about how to build connections and relationships is profound. He cuts through the tension of how some people think of networking as a 'dirty' word—the coil goes beyond networking to look at relationships more holistically. He encourages us take the risk to ask the off-the-wall question and see what may come of it."

—**Grant Duncan**, consultant

"I highly recommend this book. I was able to apply the ideas from the book right away in my every day life which has opened both personal and professional opportunities for me. It explains how you can take advantage of almost any situation you are in and really has truly enhanced the quality of my life. It's a must read!"

—**Lisa Shulman**, Kaiser

Contact the author at:
coilstories@gmail.com
coilstories.com

CONTENTS

ACKNOWLEDGEMENTS
5

INTRODUCTION
7

CHAPTER ONE
Meet the Coil
9

CHAPTER TWO
You Know More People Than You Think You Do
23

CHAPTER THREE
Not All Who Wander Are Lost
33

CHAPTER FOUR
You Miss Every Shot You Don't Take
43

CHAPTER FIVE
Unconscious Doesn't Mean Unthinking
55

CHAPTER SIX
At the End of the Day, It's All Chocolate
65

EPILOGUE
A New Story Every Day
75

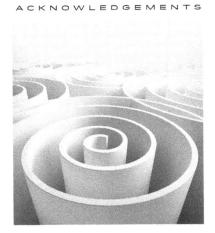

Books such as this do not happen by accident but through years of interaction with hundreds if not thousands of people. Each of these interactions enriched my life in one or more ways. My life has been complete in relationships with family, work, non-profits, education and friends. Some of those stories are reflected in this little book.

There are a few people that have been particularly encouraging to me. My wife, Antje, has been consistently encouraging to me, believing in me and the ideas in this book! Without the gently "you can do it", I would not even have undertaken the task.

Tony Thomopoulos was the first to really say, "Greg, you really need to write these ideas down." Drs. Jerry Root, Tony Payne and Jeff Davis, all professors at Wheaton College have been giving advice and encouragement for years. Lastly, I'm grateful for my fellow employees that put up with my sometimes crazy ideas and for the past twenty years the individuals and organizations that I've been privileged to work with and who have all challenged my thinking and helped me grow in so many ways.

Mostly, I am grateful for Steve Halliday. He, as a professional author and writer, agreed to come alongside me and take my ideas and thoughts and make them intelligible in writing. For that I am for ever in his debt.

This little book is not about cheese or mice, as much as I like varieties of both. It's not about monks or riddles, swimming with sharks, dancing elephants, purple cows, barbarians, flat worlds, or wise crowds. It doesn't have a red cover, give millinery advice, or encourage you to break even a few rules.

It's about a coil, a vitally important coil. *Your* coil, in fact.

I've worked with The Coil over many years now, and inevitably I've seen it prove to be a significant and even critical part of leadership success.

I can't remember exactly when I first started thinking of it as "The Coil." I used it to varying degrees long before I named it, but only after naming it did it become the life-enriching, business-enhancing, soul-fortifying force in my life that it is today.

So, what exactly is The Coil?

In brief, it's a valuable thread of personal relationships that you intentionally assemble over time, one that enriches you and others in countless ways in all aspects of your life. It's founded on the simple premise that recognizing your ability to build your own coil allows you to achieve greater results than you would otherwise enjoy.

Through these personal connections come better opportunities for *everyone* joined in some way to your coil.

The Coil is not about how many degrees of separation may exist between two people, but about total connectivity in all aspects of life. It is not merely local, regional, or national in scope, but truly international. It infuses intrigue into life, even when least expected. It's far more than networking and much more than enhancing business contacts. At its best, building your own coil becomes almost an unconscious habit that can bring a surprising richness to everything and everyone it touches.

Irrespective of where you are, where you go, or what you do, you have the ability, through The Coil, to take appropriate advantage of every opportunity and conversation that comes to you. Through The Coil, you can begin to explore a wonderful, exotic, fresh new world that most people have yet to discover. While the ways of The Coil are not always easy, yet nearly always they bring great reward—sometimes, staggeringly so.

The key question becomes, do you and I want to get connected to a broader world that gives us the amazing chance to acquire and enjoy an expanding base of knowledge and relationships? Not everyone answers that question in the affirmative. But if you are among those who say "yes!" then allow me to introduce you to The Coil.

CHAPTER 1

Meet the Coil

recently attended an advisory board meeting for a large public university. At least three times during the meeting, I heard the school's dean mention "Greg's coil." It fascinated me that our initial discussions about what I call "The Coil" already have begun to take root and make a difference in how these bright professionals think and operate.

Almost no sooner did I return home than I received an encouraging email from a very different business associate and friend in another part of the country. "I forgot to mention my favorite feel good thing of the week," he told me. "At the conference, I talked quite a bit with a couple of board members about some of my thoughts and feelings about the need for better economic soundness to integrate with their insights and social ideology. I visited one of those board members last month, and she introduced me via email to the group's interim leader. He subsequently met with me and we had a great conversation. He and another leader were talking about similar themes last week and he mentioned me to his friend. He said he feels my input was timely and he's seeking to involve me further in this issue at his organization. He's coming back to meet with me again in a couple weeks. I am excited about the chance to be part of that conversation and I'm amazed that The Coil so quickly took me from attendee to workshop speaker to being part of conversations with the group's leadership. Making an actual difference in this will be easier said than done, I'm sure, but I am eager to see what unfolds."

In both cases, these accomplished people are making far more important connections today, and doing far more with them, than they once did. They are learning to look at and interact with the world in a way far different than they used to, and that difference is positively reshaping their professional and personal lives. That is the power of The Coil.

A POTENT JOURNEY

I'm not sure how many years I've been working with The Coil, but long before I gave a name to it, I began to catch glimpses of its power. Still, only after I gave it a name did it begin to do in my life everything it has the power to do.

After I graduated from Wheaton College back in the early '70s, I began working at a national service agency with branches all over the country. I soon found myself on a fast track to upper management that brought me increasing responsibilities. The company sent me first to North Carolina and then to Colorado, assigning me various jobs for a few months at a time.

A couple of years into this, I decided to take a leave of absence in order to lead a summer sports ministry trip to Africa with two men, one of them a coach I knew from college. I didn't know the other fellow well, even though he, too, had attended Wheaton. He worked in commercial real estate, where he had done fairly well.

This coach, whom I still count as one of my dearest friends, talked often about servant leadership. Eventually I began to see several disconnects between the idea of servant leadership and what I saw happening at my company. I couldn't shake the memory of an experience I'd had with one of our janitors. He came to me one day, very agitated, and said, "Greg, I have a large family, and it's hard to take care of five kids on minimum wage. How can I make some more money?"

"I'm sorry," I answered, "there's nothing more we can do."

The very next week, the company called us in and said, "Go out and tell your people all the things we're doing really well. We're splitting shares two for one! We're making more money than we've ever made! God has really blessed us."

When I passed along this glowing report to the janitor, he replied, "So . . . what's all this *God* business?" I frankly didn't know what to say.

When I returned to the States after that summer, I tendered my resignation, even though I'd been married a little less than two years and had no clue what kind of business I wanted to be in. I felt totally discouraged.

Just then I got a call from Landey, my new friend from the Africa trip. "Greg," he said, "why don't you come down here? I think I can get you a job at the company I work for."

"Okay," I said, "I need *something*."

I visited Chicago to speak with the owners, who agreed to put me on a retainer for $1,000 a month to lease office space downtown. Understand, I didn't know a thing about real estate. I didn't know anything about leasing. I knew *nothing*. But I worked hard at it for six months.

And I absolutely failed. I didn't close one deal. I didn't even come *close* to doing one deal.

So once more, I felt totally bewildered and completely discouraged. *I just don't fit,* I thought, *and no one has offered to teach me what to do.* Landey, however, convinced his superiors that they should give me another shot. They agreed and sent me out to O'Hare Airport, where they managed a property. An older employee on site planned to retire and the owners wanted me to replace him. That man taught me a lot, and in a very short time, I found my professional niche.

About six months later, someone representing the building's owner came to me and said, "Greg, we really like what you're doing here on our property. Why don't you come work for us and do *all* of our properties?"

Wow! Such a big promotion, so soon. I enthusiastically accepted—but candidly, I failed to do right by the people who had stuck with me for all those lean months. While I've never regretted my job decision, I do regret that I paid back my former employers by taking away their business once I finally hit my stride.

I worked with the new firm for a few years, loving every minute of it. And then, out of the blue, Landey called again . . . The Coil at work once more, although I didn't recognize it. "Greg," he said, "I've learned that a company from England is coming to town. I know the guy they've hired as president and he told me they're looking for someone to do their asset management. I told him the best guy in the country was you," a total fiction. But Landey continued: "I told him he needs to talk to you, so expect a call."

Sure enough, the president called me and hired me. All of a sudden, I found myself managing what became a huge national portfolio. That call and that hire set my career on a whole new trajectory.

It didn't escape my attention that Landey didn't have anything to gain personally, either by recommending me for that first leasing job, or by sticking up for me after I so miserably failed, or by suggesting my name to the new president. I owe him a ton because he believed in me when no one else had any reason to. More than once, Landey went out of his way to use his coil to assist me at some crucial juncture. He didn't go miles out of his way, but he did have to make some conscious, intentional decisions to spend a few minutes to use his coil for the benefit of someone else.

Why'd he do that?

He did it because The Coil is all about *relationships*. It's about using what you know either to extend someone a helping hand or to give your own future an assist.

The Coil is about far more than making connections, although mere connections may morph into a coil over time. The Coil works because relationship lies at its heart.

If you were to see my Facebook or LinkedIn™ pages, you'd notice maybe a few hundred people listed as friends or contacts. Some business consultants might view my pages and say, "Wow, Greg, this surprises me. You don't seem to be all that well connected. I have five *thousand* connections on LinkedIn alone." But with very few exceptions, everyone listed on my page is someone I *know*. I don't just know *of* them; I know them and they know me. Of course, I know some of these individuals better than I know others; there are different degrees and depths of knowing. But with every connection listed, I have enjoyed some kind of *personal* interaction—very different than mere connection.

Although some coil interactions are more about ideas than people, almost inevitably, at some point I start to see how someone else is doing something similar. In that case, I usually try to suggest a relational connection that might not only enhance the idea, but also expand the person's coil. I love the challenge of trying to connect one idea to another and then seeing if I can facilitate a new person-to-person connection. In a nutshell, that's The Coil.

FROM ABSTRACT TO CONCRETE

Have you ever had some great idea that somehow failed to "stick"? It really didn't take flight for you until you connected it with some memorable image. Only then did your concept come fully to life.

Many iconic American businesses found real success only when they started using a memorable word or image to which consumers readily connected. Which of the following companies do you think you'd be more likely to choose?

➤ Quantum Computer Services? Or AmericaOnLine?

➤ Odeo? Or Twitter?

➤ Jerry's Guide to the World Wide Web? Or Yahoo?

> ➤ AuctionWeb? Or EBay?

> ➤ Confinity? Or PayPal?

Each of these companies changed its name from the first option to the second, and the name change by itself had a huge part in the firm's subsequent success. The new names succeeded in part because all of us tend to think in pictures. Do you think I'm more likely to trust a faceless corporation named Confinity to handle my personal financial transactions, or a pal who offers to pay someone for me?

Many modern linguists believe that *all* language is essentially metaphorical—that is, we connect nearly everything we discuss to some form of picture, image, or symbol, so that even our abstract thoughts are grounded in something much more tangible. The simpler and easier those pictures are to remember, the more we tend to use the ideas connected to those pictures.

I mentioned earlier that while The Coil helped me long before I named it, it's profited me in far greater ways since I've given it a name. Naming it and associating it with a simple, potent picture has given the thing a vibrant life of its own. Not surprisingly, I've seen this happen countless times in the lives of friends, associates, and clients. If you want the power of The Coil to work for you, you need to pair the concept with a picture and a name.

A metaphor like "The Coil" does more than act as a shorthand way to refer to something larger or more complex than itself. It quite literally takes on a life of its own. It shapes how we think and act. We behave differently because of the metaphor than we would if we didn't have it in our heads. I like what English authors, Michael Berman and David Brown, have written in their book, *The Power of Metaphor:*

> It has been suggested that if a picture is worth a thousand words, then perhaps we can regard a metaphor as being worth 1000 pictures. According to psychologists, our memories seem to work best when we can see things as part of a recognised pattern, when our imaginations are aroused, when we can make natural associations between

one idea and another, and when the information appeals strongly to our senses. (p. 4, *The Power of Metaphor*, Michael Berman and David Brown, 2005, Crown House Publishing Limited: Carmarthen, Wales)

When I consider The Coil, I think not merely of an interesting concept, but I see a mental picture that prompts me to grow and nurture and expand the relationships I develop through a variety of settings. In fact, the image not only helps me "get" the idea, but actually reminds me and motivates me to consistently apply the concept in my life, so that it positively *improves* my life. The picture of The Coil moves me to action, rather than just giving me a nice intellectual handle to grasp the idea. The physical picture of a coil spurs me and influences me to change the way I behave, and in the process enriches my life in a million unanticipated ways.

When you start thinking about building your own coil—when that picture of the physical thing sets up shop in your mind—then you'll be far more likely to actually build your coil than if you merely thought it'd be nice to get to know a few more people sometime. You'll be far more likely to build it than if you just thought, *Yes, that's an interesting idea, but I've heard something like it before.* Metaphors, remember, have the power to change lives. So why not start using that power to change your own?

Part of the trick is to start thinking of your own coil rather than just as "Greg's coil." It'll start to work its magic best when you own The Coil as yours, not merely admire it as mine. I'm about to tell you how I hit on the image of a coil, to help you see why that picture is so potent for me. If the same picture doesn't grab you, then find a picture that does. Without that picture in your head, however, I know you won't pursue or experience the amazing benefits that The Coil has for you. I love "the coil" because it's a simple, memorable, concrete, and short word that's easy to say out loud. The image of a coil works best for me and for many others. Here's why.

SEARCHING FOR A PICTURE

When most of us think about how personal connections get made, we typically conjure up images like the wake behind a boat.

I've owned a boat for many years, so I "get" the image of a wake generating an ever-widening sweep of influence. But once the wake travels some distance from the boat, can I *really* understand how my wake has influenced others, or been influenced by them? In my opinion, the wake illustration doesn't clearly show how my influence on one person ends up influencing another, and then a third and a fourth. It doesn't fully picture the impact of the connectivity of our relationships and our ability to use those relationships and connections in a potent, appropriate way.

When I began searching for a better image to more accurately picture this phenomenon, I had a great conversation with Dr. Jerry Root, one of my closest friends. He suggested the image of a helix, a smooth curve that functions in three dimensional space, not unlike a spiral ramp.

When I later spoke to my daughter about the idea, she immediately thought of a Slinky, a toy helical spring that stretches and can bounce up and down. One of the Slinky's unique features is its ability to stretch and reform itself and to "walk" downstairs on its own power.

While both of these suggestions have merit, however, they touch on only a single understanding of the total experience I had in mind. Neither suggestion captured the full intent of my premise.

So I started scribbling. Eventually I drew a poorly-executed coil, intersecting with another coil. "This is me," I said, pointing to one coil, "and this is someone else," pointing to the second coil. I noted the various points of intersection between the two coils and declared, "It's something like this."

A coil "works" as a metaphor because different coils can intersect at different levels and at multiple points. They're not circles; they're not even elliptical, necessarily. They can be a little bit of everything.

Picture a sawn-off tree trunk. A tree's growth rings vary from year to year; some are big and some are small. They don't all look the same.

In a similar way, a coil lacks a uniform appearance. Its shape and length and volume may vary through time. Separate coils overlap at various points and may even go backwards and forwards. The Coil starts with small, tight circles, becoming larger and, sometimes, elliptical. The width of The Coil may grow thicker or thinner. It is continuous and very traceable from its starting point (birth) to its current position.

The image of a coil gives us an easy way to discuss, categorize, and "file" the varied stories that emerge as our lives intersect. When we use our coils thoughtfully, they can bring us to places of helpful reflection, not obsession.

Reflect back on your own life. Your experiences did not grow at the same pace nor at the same level of detail, year by year. The Coil by necessity starts small with tight circles. As your life experiences move you forward, it becomes larger. The width of the coil may grow thicker or thinner at different periods, representing the depth as well as the breadth of your experiences.

As your coil expands, you intersect with a very large number of other coils. The question then becomes how and where your coil intersects with those others. And at each point of intersection, for whatever period of time the connection lasts, the question becomes, how does that intersection help you and others move toward the life goals you all have?

Look at the two coils pictured on page 18, the top image is the day my own coil began. I can find a flow back through my whole life to every connection I've ever had, beginning with my birth. Nothing else that I know of has that capacity. Your coil has a different starting point than mine, a different date of birth. Suppose that our lives have intersected; maybe we have a mutual friend that made that happen. The more time we spend together, the more we do with one another. So while the depth of our relationship is larger than it is with the friend, the area of intersection between you and your friend may be much bigger than ours. This kind of graphic, displaying elliptical, concentric shapes, illustrates the many kinds of value connections we may have.

MORE THAN SIX DEGREES

Many years ago, a friend sent me an article from the very first edition of *Psychology Today*. Stanley Milgram had written an intriguing piece titled, "The Small World Problem." Although I had not read or even heard of the article (from May 1967), it very clearly speaks to the message of The Coil as I have come to understand it. Milgram wrote:

> Fred Jones of Peoria, sitting in a sidewalk café in Tunisia, and needing a light for his cigarette, asks the man at the next table for a match. They fall into a conversation; the stranger is an Englishman who, it turns out, spent several months in Detroit studying the operation of an interchangeable bottle factory.
>
> "I know it's a foolish question," says Jones, "but did you ever by any chance run into a fellow named Ben Arcadian? He's an old friend of mine, manages a chain of supermarkets in Detroit."
>
> "Arcadian . . . Arcadian," the Englishman mutters. "Why, upon my soul, I believe I do! Small chap, very energetic, raised merry hell with the factory over a shipment of defective bottle caps."

"No kidding!" Jones exclaims, amazed. "Good lord, it's a small world, isn't it?"

Milgram's article and subsequent work inspired the phrase "six degrees of separation," the idea that we can find a connection to any other individual in America through a chain of half a dozen personal ties. This idea eventually sparked the "Six Degrees of Kevin Bacon" game, in which players try to identify a connection to the famous actor through a series of six or fewer acquaintances.

While I appreciate and want to take advantage of such connections, however, The Coil is not just another way of saying, "it's a small world, isn't it?" In fact, when you put your coil to work, you leverage these "small world" moments for the benefit of many, not the least of which is yourself.

Nor is The Coil just another way of talking about networking. Most of us tend to think of networking as the process of making connections with others who can help us to find a good job or to build a larger pool of professional contacts. We want to expand our network so we can get another sale, locate a better supplier, or progress toward some specific professional objective. Networking, in other words, tends to focus very specifically on some aspect of business.

As I write, my nephew is going through a job search. Imagine that he identifies a prospective employer. Suppose he searches LinkedIn by company name and asks every executive he can find there to connect with him. And perhaps he then sends a few of these execs his resume. His strategy could net him a job with a really fine company, so I'd consider it a useful tool.

Is that networking? Certainly. Is it an example of The Coil? Not really.

The Coil has a much broader, wider, and all-encompassing purpose. While The Coil may include business, it goes far beyond business to embrace the personal and even spiritual realms. The Coil is a whole-life enterprise built around inquisitiveness and intentionality, all designed to bring a variety of benefits to everyone it touches.

KEY BENEFITS OF YOUR COIL

Let me briefly list a few of the most important benefits of developing your own coil. If you choose to put it to work for you, you can expect to enjoy:

> *Increased confidence.* Intentionally using your coil makes it far easier for you to "break the ice" in uncomfortable social situations, allowing you and everyone else to relax.

> *Unlimited learning opportunities.* Stoking your curiosity about the world inevitably expands your knowledge base, which exponentially increases your ability to handle unexpected situations.

> *Improved self-image.* By habitually using your coil to expand what you know, along with your ability to help others, you strengthen your self-image and equip yourself to enjoy life more fully.

> *Enlarged business options.* When you use your coil to take you into uncharted territory, you make important connections that can benefit both your business and the interests of the individuals in your expanding world.

> *Occasions to help others.* Since The Coil is as much about giving as it is getting, by tapping its power you gain the ability to assist others in practical and often surprising ways. Joy often breaks out.

> *Heightened self-awareness.* The Coil works best when you learn to take careful note of your surroundings and of the individuals around you, thus fostering a heightened self-awareness that significantly improves your day-to-day experience.

> *More fun.* Life simply becomes more fun when you train yourself to take advantage of all the opportunities afforded by a well-used coil.

In the past few weeks, I've seen a remarkable coil story unfold in my own family. As I write, my adult son is facing serious open heart surgery. I put my coil into play when I called an old friend, a highly regarded cardiologist from Stanford. Did he have any suggestions on good surgeons in our area? My friend gave me a name. A little later, I emailed a few friends with news about the surgery, and one of them, traveling in New Zealand, told me that his son's father-in-law served as the lead heart surgeon at USC, a physician widely considered the best surgeon in Southern California. My traveling friend mentioned exactly the same name as did my Stanford friend.

This connection alone would have been enough for me, but my coil then continued to work its magic (as it often does). My son quickly got an appointment with the recommended surgeon, an appointment made possible only through my traveling friend's daughter-in-law; we couldn't have reached the busy doctor in any other way. And just recently we discovered that the surgeon's daughter and my daughter-in-law once taught at the same school. A classic coil story!

Sometimes, the benefits of The Coil are interesting. Sometimes, they're vitally important. And sometimes, they're just plain fun. But always they're worthwhile.

Even if you think you don't have a coil.

CHAPTER 2

You Know More People Than You Think You Do

I hope you like short chapters, because this is one. It has only a single main point, which you've read already if you scanned the title:

You know more people than you think you do.

Despite its brevity, the idea is crucial enough to warrant a chapter of its own, because so many people I meet struggle tremendously with its truth. They just don't believe it. And therefore, should a time come when they have to make a major life change, they start to worry. Some get deeply discouraged, even to the point of depression. Others simply panic. All of them have essentially the same fear: "What if nobody wants me?"

I know that sounds sad; but do you know the *really* sad (and extremely surprising) part of the story? It doesn't matter if the person had a blue collar job or occupied a penthouse corner suite. It doesn't matter if the individual oversaw 20,000 employees or none. And it doesn't matter if he or she worked in the private sector, the public sector, or in some kind of tax exempt ministry or public service organization. Once these anxious individuals start talking to me about their situation, all of them nearly always say the same thing in almost the same words: "I don't know anybody who wants me!"

And to all of them, I almost always say the same thing in nearly the same words: "I beg to differ."

WHO MIGHT WANT ME?

Not long ago, a bright man with an impressive résumé and a long track record of major success sought me out when he had to change careers. Tens of thousands of men and women reported to him and he'd risen in the organization almost as high as he could go. What it would take for him to make the final leap to the top, however, didn't appeal to him, and he felt certain he could not long remain in his strategic position. An associate of his had given him my name and number and said, "Call Greg."

He did, although without a great deal of enthusiasm. When he described his background and the kind of assignments he'd successfully pulled off, it almost took away my breath. I thought, *this guy is golden*. And then he said it.

"I don't have many contacts outside of my current job," he stated, glumly. "Do you think anyone would have any interest in me?" He paused. "I can't think of anyone."

I felt almost like shouting, "ARE YOU *KIDDING ME?!?*" But of course, I muted my impulse. I'd heard the same story too many times already to feel totally surprised by it. Nearly all of us, deep down, try to keep at bay a secret and gnawing fear that we don't measure up, that we don't know many people willing to help us, and that we're headed directly toward the trash heap.

It isn't true, of course. But very often, that's what we think. And rank and status and success and accolades seem to have very little power to make us think otherwise.

Joe Castleberry's recent book, The Kingdom Net, reminded me of this peculiar fact. Toward the end of his book, he speaks about Kendra VanderMeulen, president of the National Christian Foundation in Seattle, Washington. He calls her "nothing less than a business superwoman" and lists part of her professional background: President of AT&T's Conversant Systems, Senior Vice-President and General Manager of the Wireless Data Division of AT&T Wireless, Executive Vice President (Mobile) at InfoSpace, and a board member of several organizations, including B-Square, Inrix, Perlego Systems, and Soul-Formation.

That's quite a résumé (and only a partial one)! But shortly after the 911 terrorist attacks, the tech bubble burst, Kendra lost half her net worth, and she found herself unemployed. No problem for someone like her, right? But that's not what she thought. Without a job or a compelling purpose, she remembers feeling "scared out of my mind" and wondering, *Will I ever matter again in this world?*[1]

It's possible you might be feeling a lot like that, right now. Regardless of your background or professional accomplishments, you can see the day fast approaching when you may need to make a new start—and the very thought worries you, scares you, maybe even paralyzes you.

Does anybody want you? Who out there might be willing to help you find a new job or identify a new purpose? Where and how do you start to build a new future?

While the specific process plays out differently for every individual, I always recommend that everyone start in the same place: Your coil. You may believe you don't know many people who have the ability or the willingness to help, but I can almost guarantee that you're wrong. You really do know more people than you think you do.

---

[1] Joseph Castleberry, *The Kingdom Net.* (Springfield, MO: My Healthy Church, 2013), 273-279

BROADER THAN YOU THINK

Everyone has a coil, even if they've never called it that. It may be underdeveloped, it may not get a lot of use, but it exists. And that's where you start.

Your coil is much broader than everyone in your contact list, plus your friends on Facebook, plus your connections on LinkedIn. Remember, your coil started with your birth and continues until this very moment. Everyone who has personally touched your life in some way has a place on your coil, whether a tiny spot or a mammoth swath.

While I don't recommend that you try to create an exhaustive list of everyone on your coil (it would take too long, waste a lot of time, and I don't think you could do it, anyway), I do suggest that you sit down someplace quiet and write down the names of the individuals who had the greatest impact on you. Maybe you could divide your list into a few sections (e.g., early life, teen years, college, career, etc.) or perhaps into decades. Who on that list is still living? Whose contact information do you still have? What sort of connections do you believe these people might have? Just start compiling a list of the significant people you know, and of the significant people you believe your contacts may know. This is a part of your own coil.

Even those who feel convinced they have a very small world and very few key connections inevitably know more people than they think they do. Sitting down and trying to take conscious stock of even this small part of your coil enables you to begin identifying that larger world. Once you've done that, the real work of The Coil begins. You have to be willing to listen, observe, learn, take a risk, and reach out, both for your own benefit and to bless others. Over and over again, I've seen how tapping into their coil helps men and women gain in confidence and reduce their insecurity. And all of them who do so inevitably learn the main point of this chapter: *I know more people than I thought I did.* What's more, they discover that most people are willing to help, at least in small ways.

Years ago, after I had begun to formulate my thoughts on The Coil, I began testing my ideas. Once I went to a cocktail party in California, sponsored by a large bank that had invited customers from all around the United States. I first thought it unlikely that I would know anyone there other than bank staff. But I decided to test my developing premise. I wondered how long it would take before I met someone whom either I knew, or who knew a third party familiar to both of us. I decided to make a game out of it.

The very first couple I spoke to told me they had come to the party from Florida. The man casually said that he and his wife also owned a home in Grand Rapids, Michigan. With that little clue in hand, I asked him, "By any chance, might you know Bob Smith? He owns a small manufacturing company there. He was my college roommate and has been a lifelong friend."

The man brightened and immediately replied, "Why, yes. I've known the family for two generations and have done significant business with them."

In less than five minutes, I had used the strategy of asking off-the-wall questions to discover that my coil, which many years before had intersected with that of my college friend, had now intersected with the coil of this man from Florida.

Five minutes.

Now, I'm not a particularly gregarious person. No one has ever accused me of being a social butterfly. I don't naturally flit from individual to individual, effortlessly establishing interpersonal connections as easily as TV's current *Bachelor* lands exotic dates from the bevy of beautiful women recruited for that purpose. It takes conscious effort to listen, observe, assess, risk the asking of wild (but contextualized) questions, and then seeing if I can make a connection.

And yet, at that California cocktail party so many years ago . . . *five minutes.*

I'm pretty sure you can do at least that well.

TO HELP A HEAD HUNTER,
USE YOUR HEAD

Most of this chapter has revolved around using your coil to pave the way for creating a new future, a legitimate use of your coil. But I don't want to move to the next chapter without reiterating that The Coil exists equally to afford us opportunities to help others. It's reciprocal.

Several years ago, I got a call from a head hunter looking for someone to run GMAC home services, owned at the time by General Motors. The man wanted names of viable candidates; he knew I wasn't in the market. An acquaintance immediately came to mind. But I asked, "Who are you talking to already?" The man named one individual who had worked for me in the past, a man I valued very highly. *He is as good as you can get,* I thought. But I'd also worked with the man I'd just recalled, and I believed that he might be an even better fit for the job.

I call this "coiling back around." But The Coil is about more than mere facts; it's also about evaluation, assessment, appraisal. *I know both of these players,* I thought. *I know both of their work. And I'm starting to understand the need of this company. In my judgment, the man I thought of first might work out better than the man the head hunter already has spoken to.*

So I told the head hunter, "The man you mentioned is a great candidate. I know him personally and he's really good. But I also know another man who might suit the needs of the company even better. He might be what you really need."

The man I recommended for the position ended up getting hired, and he did a wonderful job for that company. But the story ended well for the other man, too; a little while later, he became president of a large and influential international real estate corporation, which was a much more appropriate fit for his skill set.

Notice how The Coil worked in favor of both men. Each one got a major executive job. While I used my influence in a minor way to help one of them get a great position, my "negative" influence in regard to the other person helped paved the way for him to seize a different opportunity, one that suited him much better.

As a result of that phone call, I began to see that my relationships and my understanding of the real estate business could be leveraged to help others in ways that had nothing to do with benefitting my own personal interests. I also started to grasp more clearly than I had before that using what I later came to call The Coil was not just about fact, but about assessment, about thoughtfully connecting, about trying to make sense out of the data I knew and the connections I had, and then taking some risk to put my thoughts on the table.

THE CHITS SAVINGS & LOAN

As I think about a term like "leveraging," my mind naturally travels to the world of finance and numbers. And what says "numbers" and "finance" better than a bank or a savings & loan?

As we intersect with many people over the course of our lives, whether for a short term or a much longer period, we build up what we might term "relationship points" with these individuals. Better yet, let's call these relationship points "chits." Chits are a form of relational currency we keep safe in a bank. What we invest in the bank is meant for future use, to be withdrawn only after we exercise a fair amount of discretion regarding their appropriate expenditure. We will not withdraw our chits indiscriminately.

We build up our account in the Chits Savings & Loan through our positive interactions with the individuals we encounter along our coil. The larger our account grows, the more potential we have to accomplish some important future ventures, funded in part by making appropriate withdrawals. Every person on The Coil has some kind of chits account. At different times and in different ways, others may call on me for a withdrawal from the account I'm holding for them.

How do we go about helping each other on The Coil? How do I assist you in your endeavors to be more productive and successful? The most important thing to remember is that when someone in our

coil calls upon us to make a withdrawal from our savings account, we respond by doing whatever we can, "just because." We must have no expectation of reciprocity. At the same time, we must be prepared for the same thing when we call upon someone else to make a withdrawal from their account.

I realize that, to many, this concept may seem counterproductive or even inappropriate. It may smack of "using" someone. But that is never the intent. There is an enormous difference between using someone inappropriately and coming alongside to help an individual who needs the help.

While the metaphor of the chit helps me to appreciate what often happens through The Coil, like most metaphors and analogies, it only approximates the reality. A strident demand that the withdrawal of ten chits requires a later deposit of exactly ten chits will almost certainly lead to disappointment, resentment, and anger. The Coil just doesn't work that way. Still, the idea of a Chits Saving & Loan does speak to the reciprocal nature of The Coil, which works best in the spirit of give and take, not demand and yield.

A GOLDEN CONCLUSION

Remember the "golden" man from the beginning of this chapter who thought he had few viable connections outside of his longtime profession? In fact, he made quite the opposite discovery.

It turned out, of course, he knew a lot more people than he thought he did.

This man and I had many conversations about his coil and about his existing connections (far more than he'd realized). With some focused work on his part and by taking some small risks, he soon discovered that he had many broad-based connections. As he began to connect with these people whom he had labored to identify, he also discovered (as so many others have) how willing most people are to give of their time. He found that while these coil connections might not lead to a new job or to any new specific professional opportunity, they always left him more confident in his ability to find meaningful work and feeling more positive about his future.

Of course, The Coil also can be phenomenal at helping people find excellent jobs. It certainly turned out that way for this man. Even as I write, he's enjoying a new challenge in a business that suits him very well. He loves his job and his confidence has soared.

And I think it's safe to say he would count himself a firm believer in the surprising power of The Coil.

QUESTIONS, QUESTIONS

I know The Coil can help men and women find options for their futures, even if they doubt they know anybody who might be willing to help them. But the Coil is about more than that. *Much* more.

It's about becoming better.

If I have any interest at all in becoming something better than what I already am, then how can I *not* be interested in The Coil? Only if I want to live in isolation—and I know of some individuals who want exactly that—will I fail to have any curiosity about what The Coil could do for and in me. I want to know how I can leverage, in all aspects of life, the remarkable power of The Coil to make me into a better person.

I love to learn new things that might make my world a little better. I want to know what's happening around me. And since I've learned that a healthy dose of curiosity fuels The Coil, I want to feed that curiosity.

Which means that a little wandering might do us all some good.

CHAPTER 3

Not All Who Wander Are Lost

My wife and I once attended a large conference in Cape Town, South Africa. I had connections with several people there and knew many attendees quite well. Antje, however, wondered whether she'd know anyone.

But within minutes of our arrival, she ran into a long-lost friend. Later, as she waited to reconnect with me, she noticed the name badge of a conference attendee, a lawyer from Ethiopia. Antje immediately started asking the kinds of questions that lead toward the possibility of a connected coil. She knew only one person in Ethiopia, a German friend of hers who had married an Ethiopian. "The couple lives in Addis Ababa," Antje said, "where they do business. Is it possible you've ever run into them?"

"Of course I know them," responded the Ethiopian. "The man is my cousin."

I find that fascinating. Someone from California with ties to Germany connected to Ethiopia while visiting South Africa. That is the surprising power of The Coil.

But notice that *none of it would have happened* without Antje's willingness to risk asking a stranger a few questions in order to find a possible connection.

A WINDING ROAD

One of the most important things to understand about our coils is that they aren't straight lines, but winding ones. They're more like rivers than freeways, more a flare than a laser. A coil can meander and zigzag and often look as if it's about to head in one direction when it suddenly curves around to shoot off somewhere else entirely. If you want to build and benefit from your own coil, then, you have to be willing to do some intentional wandering.

Imagine yourself tiny enough to go for a walk on an actual, physical coil. From your miniscule vantage point, you probably can't see where the path leads. You don't know whether it will march straight ahead, turn to the right, curve to the left, go up, down, or double back. To successfully walk that coil, you must commit yourself to some intentional wandering. It's intentional, because you consciously choose to follow it wherever it might lead. It's wandering, because you willingly follow the twisty course wherever it goes, without insisting that it get you from A to B by the shortest route possible.

"But that's such a waste of time!" someone says. And she might be right—but only if she believes that learning new things and growing in unexpected ways lacks any potential to enhance her life or benefit others. I don't claim that The Coil is for everyone! But for those who want to take a chance that doing a little intentional wandering could lead them to uncover a few hidden gems along the trail, it's actually quite exciting.

GET YOUR ANTENNAE UP

You can buy the most expensive smart phone in the world, but unless it has some sort of antenna, it will do you no good as a connecting device. You might be able to play games on it or turn it into an incredibly spendy flashlight, but that's not why you buy it. For the device to be of any value to you, it has to have some kind of antenna that can effectively capture radio signals from nearby cell phone towers.

In a similar way, the person who wants to tap the power of The Coil has to put up his or her antenna in order to capture the signals broadcast by nearby individuals. These signals might be faint or strong, clear or garbled. An effective user of The Coil listens for important clues, notes important words, hears tone of voice, watches body language, and observes how one person relates to another.

We become alert to possible connections primarily by putting up our antennae. We carefully process what we hear and what we observe and then we take a risk by asking thoughtful questions designed to see if we might connect.

For this to work, we have to remain alert for clues. We must keep our minds open to whatever hints may come, however and whenever they might arrive. Sometimes it's a name. Sometimes it's an accent. Sometimes it's a job reference. Sometimes it's a mention of a city, country or region. Sometimes it refers to a hobby or a favorite activity.

Six of us recently sat at our dining room table for a pleasant meal and some serious conversation. A very bright woman sat across the table from me. In addition to paying attention to my main conversation partner, I also tried to observe, out of the corner of my eye, how this woman seemed to react to it all. When I sensed her remaining very quiet, I took a peek—and I saw on her face a hint of consternation.

At a break in the conversation, I turned to her and said, "Susan, you've been really quiet, but I can sense you have something really important you want to say." Only at that point did she speak her mind. Now, I could have ignored what my antenna picked up. I could have dismissed her silence. Had I done so, I doubt she would have opened up—and our conversation would have been much the poorer.

Getting your antenna up involves trying to observe the connections between people. You carefully listen for words and the tone in which they're spoken. You watch body language and observe the nature of personal interactions. And then you try to tie together what you see and hear in an effort to gauge whether you might pursue some interesting coil connection. In that way, you prepare yourself for the next critical step.

ASK APPROPRIATE QUESTIONS

Once I've listened and observed enough to get a sense of the person (or of the circumstances), I often say something like, "I really doubt this could be the case, but I wonder if you might know _____?"

The key to expanding your coil is learning to ask appropriate questions, contextualized to the situation.

This doesn't "just happen." You have to be proactive about it. It's not just that you meet someone interesting and your ensuing conversation reminds you of what a small world we live in. No, to make a genuine coil conversation really take off, you have to risk a little, conduct a little impromptu investigation, and ask a few appropriate questions.

When you hear some piece of a conversation that really intrigues you, how often do you take the risk to say, "What you just said is very interesting. Would you happen to know ____?" Most of us seldom bother to pursue the intriguing line of thought; it's easier just to let it pass.

Whenever I hear friends and colleagues asking good questions, I try to affirm them. "Did you see how that worked?" I may say later. "I had no idea that such a great connection was even there. Who knows where it might lead?"

When you choose to take such a risk, listen for clues to guide your questions. *What's this person's name? Where has he lived? What kind of jobs has she had? What's his family background? When did she graduate?*

"Oh, you're German," I may say. "My wife is German, too. What part of Germany are you from?" And I let the inquisitive part of me take center stage.

When your question establishes some kind of unanticipated personal connection, the person frequently says things like, "That is *so* interesting!" And then you're off and running.

Some time ago I met a man who told me he'd worked at Raytheon. I knew only one person who'd worked there, but it was someone who had become fairly well-known within that huge corporation. So I chose to ask an off-the-wall question: "By chance," I said, "do you possibly know _____?" As soon as I mentioned the person's name, the man's whole demeanor changed. He lit up. "Yes!" he said, smiling broadly. "In fact, she once expressed an interest in hiring me! But I chose to go in another direction."

He then told me that the man she hired eventually became her boss. And I could almost see the wheels churning in his head: *What if I had taken that job? Would I have become her boss? How would my life have turned out differently?* Because I chose to ask an off-the-wall question, that man found himself in a whole new place—a very pleasant one, it seemed to me.

Asking appropriate questions tends to strongly affirm people, and we all need authentic affirmation, from top executives to summer interns. We all like to hear people say, "You sound like such a fascinating person! Tell me more!" It is highly unlikely that anyone will ever take offense at you for asking appropriate questions.

One of my favorite questions is this: "Would you help me to understand?" If I'm listening carefully and I hear something intriguing, I'm completely willing to acknowledge that I may not fully understand. When I make such a request, the words themselves are usually less important than the tone in which I deliver them. It's not as though I'm saying, "I'm sorry, but I'm a moron. C-A-N Y-O-U P-L-E-A-S-E S-P-E-A-K M-O-R-E S-L-O-W-L-Y F-O-R M-E S-O T-H-A-T I C-A-N G-E-T I-T?"

Framing our questions in this way reveals us as vulnerable, a vitally important aspect of most relationships. But just as important, it affirms others both for who they are and for what they know. Several other lead-in questions can accomplish the same thing:

"I'm just curious...."

"I was just wondering...."

"Have I heard correctly that . . . ."

Our questions need to reveal that we've been listening carefully. If I'm in a business context, I'm not likely to ask, "Have you ever played cello at the New York Met?" We need to contextualize our questions to our current circumstances, and good contextualization requires good listening and careful observation. If we're not sensitive to the signals others broadcast, we can try to go places they don't want to go, or become so self-absorbed that we remain virtually unaware of the responses we get.

DOES IT SCARE US?

Some individuals shrink back from developing their own coil out of fear. Many of us, perhaps most of us, harbor some painful insecurities that lie at our very core. We don't know where we fit in, especially in groups. So whenever we get together with a group, we try to assess our place in it: "Where do I fit, compared to this person? Where am I on the social pecking order?" It's a sad part of who we are.

While some of us have a greater ability to mask our insecurity than others, the reality remains. I see it in myself. I've worked hard over the years to overcome my core insecurities, but I know there're still there.

It's something like shingles. If you've ever had the chicken pox, the virus that causes shingles lives hidden within you. In one of every three adults, however, that virus eventually causes shingles—a painful, unsightly illness that often puts its victims in bed for weeks on end.

Our fear of The Coil is something like that. Many of us fear it because we think, consciously or subconsciously, *Relationships scare me. I can handle chains of command. I can flourish in my office. But I don't want anybody to get too close. If people knew the "real me," they'd get as far away as possible.*

One of the great things about developing your own coil, however, is that once you start listening, observing, evaluating, asking questions, and expecting to grow in surprising ways, you start to gain confidence. At the very least, you end up knowing something that you didn't know before. And even a little increase in unexpected knowledge can feel pretty good, can't it?

WHAT'S WRONG WITH FEELING GOOD?

Something really good usually happens inside of us when we choose to develop our coils. Wonderful things begin to take place physiologically.

In response to stimuli such pain, stress, and vigorous exercise, our bodies release a class of specialized neurotransmitters called endorphins, morphine-like substances that both block pain and generate feelings of pleasure. The human body produces at least twenty types of endorphins, and while the amount released varies from individual to individual, these opioid compounds are responsible for anything from the famed "runner's high" to the pleasant feelings we get when we reconnect with an old friend.

While we can't physically transfer endorphins from one person to another, our actions can spur the release of endorphins in others. The individuals we help certainly experience pleasant feelings, and sometimes bystanders who observe one person helping another also get an "endorphin rush."

Of course, it would be very easy to circumvent all of this endorphin releasing. All you have to do is . . . nothing. All it takes is a decision not to engage your coil, to avoid taking the risk. Who expects you to ask off-the-wall questions? No law requires you to speak. The question is, is the risk "worth it"?

And I think you already know my answer.

SURPRISE, SURPRISE

A friend of mine, Jim, has done "networking" for many years, but only recently has begun to do so with The Coil in mind. He tells me that the metaphor itself has helped him to focus his efforts and get more out of his interactions. He gave me a recent example.

Jim speaks occasionally at retreats and seminars, and at a recent engagement, the man who booked him for the event wanted to get a little personal information for an introduction. Instead of giving the man only what he requested, however, Jim started asking him about his own life. Part of the conversation went like this:

Jim: "You said you're not originally from this area. Where did you grow up?"

Man: "I grew up in a little town in Minnesota that nobody's ever heard of."

"Really? My parents were originally from Minnesota, and they spent about a decade of their final years in small town named Babbitt."

"It gets cold up there!"

"Yes, it does. Right after they moved, I was listening to a radio station and heard that it got to 60 below in Tower, just a few miles from their home."

"Tower? That's really close to my home town, Soudan."

"No kidding? I was just through Soudan a couple of weeks ago, visiting my sister. She and her husband like to camp at a place right on Lake Vermillion."

"Do you mean McKinley Park?"

"Why, yes, I think that's the name."

"That's unbelievable! Nobody's ever heard of Soudan, Minnesota, let alone McKinley Park!"

Jim told me that this short conversation provided a perfect bridge to his presentation and helped him connect with the members of a group who before that time had been perfect strangers to him.

Take a risk! Ask some questions! Wander a bit. And then let your coil do its thing.

CHAPTER 4

You Miss Every Shot
You Don't Take

A successful businessman once asked if I might help him increase his professional reach. The two of us discussed several concepts regarding The Coil and how he might leverage, in a proactive and positive way, what he already had in order to achieve even greater good. I encouraged him to begin reconnecting with people from his past who had been part of his coil. I suggested he explain to them some of his vocational desires and needs, given that he wanted to expand his work to a larger area.

"Why would these people want to talk to *me*?" he asked, clearly hesitant to follow my advice. I urged him to give it a try anyway.

Several days later, he called to say, "Greg, this really *works*. I have been surprised and grateful by the responses I've been getting from people. They not only take my call, they *want* to help in any way they can."

The same man often has significant downtime because of his travel and speaking schedule. So a short while later I asked him, "When you visit a city, what do you do between speaking engagements? What do you do with your downtime?"

"Well, I usually go to the hotel," he replied. "And I write. Or I prepare for some other speaking engagement."

"Here's something you might want to consider," I answered. "You spend a lot of both money and time to get to some place where you're trying to build your connections and your business, right?"

"Yes."

"So, why do you retreat into a box when you're there?"

I didn't want him to overdo it, of course, because he has to be physically and mentally prepared to do whatever he came to town to do. But I did want him to get in the habit of asking, "Who else could I meet with while I'm in town? How could I use my downtime to reconnect with former contacts and work toward achieving my expansion goals?"

When he took my suggestion—this time, with significantly more enthusiasm than before—he found many more opportunities to advance his business and deepen his personal relationships. The strategy also has led to several new friendships and to a broader understanding of the larger world he inhabits. And isn't that the point?

His experience demonstrates that to tap the power of your own coil, you must be both proactive and intentional. It won't "just happen." Hockey great Wayne Gretzky once famously said, "You miss 100 percent of the shots you don't take," and his sage advice is as relevant to The Coil as it is to the hockey rink. You'll never score a goal unless you wind up and take a shot. In other words, recognizing and *acting* on your ability to build your coil allows you to achieve greater results than you can otherwise enjoy.

PROACTIVE DOESN'T HAVE TO
MEAN NARROWLY FOCUSED

None of us knows what we don't know. One of the dangers I see in much of contemporary online education is that it often doesn't expose students to anything other than what they think they want to know. Too much of higher education is threatening to become far too utilitarian for my tastes, with young men and women who lack deep exposure to the wide variety of the world's treasures neverthe-less choosing courses of study exclusively focused on some very nar-row and particularized field. But how will you ever know what a great architect you could become if all you study is how to play the tuba (and yes, I do hear the old *Seinfeld* mantra: "Not that there's anything wrong with that")?

Focus is great, so long as you know what you ought to focus on.

But very often, we don't know. How *can* we know, if we lack either a decent grasp of who we are as individuals or a substantial idea of the enormous range of wonders available to us "out there"? The only way to really know is to look around; and most of the time, that requires a wide angle lens rather than a telephoto lens (or a microscope).

More often than not, we ought to come to our coil wondering "what's out there?" rather than demanding that it show us the interior of a Martian crater or the cilia of a laboratory protozoan. We come to it, in other words, with very few preconceptions about what it must bring to us. While we may at times wish to tap the power of our coil for some narrowly-focused purpose—let's say, a job search—we ought to come to it most of the time for the sheer pleasure of experi-encing whatever it may happen to send our way.

We consciously choose to listen, to observe, to risk, to ask, and to assess, not to have the answer to the fifth question on tomorrow's quiz in American national politics, but to gain a better idea of the range of quizzes human beings all over the world take every day.

PROACTIVE DOESN'T HAVE TO MEAN LONG AND INVOLVED

I recently picked up a friend at the airport. As I waited for him, I decided to call a mutual friend in another city. I didn't have to call him; I had no particular agenda in mind. I could have said to myself, "Hey, I have only five minutes. It's a good thought, but not worth it." Instead, I chose to make the call.

I didn't know I'd still be on the phone when I saw my friend step out of the terminal. I hadn't planned it that way. But it worked out nicely, because the friend I came to pick up and the friend I called then got to reconnect with each other through a short, unplanned phone conversation.

Will anything come of that? Who knows? That's not the point. The point is that even brief excursions on your coil can serve to reawaken inert relationships, rekindle old friendships, and give total strangers an unexpected lift. Sometimes, you consciously tap the power of your coil for no other reason than to try to make someone's day brighter. That's an important part of what it does, and that's why I urge others to "take the shot."

I recall a true story of a brief, here-and-gone-again moment that I'm sure will stay with one woman (and probably tens of thousands of other men and women) for a very long time. Shanell Mouland, a mom with her hands full, boarded a plane with her autistic three-year-old. She dreaded the flight. She purposefully placed her daughter in the middle seat, hoping that such a strategy might be less of a distraction for a stranger than observing her daughter, Kate, open and close the window shade throughout their time in the air. She hoped that a grandmotherly type might sit in the aisle seat, but feared the worst when a well-dressed businessman sat down instead.

"I had a vision of Kate pouring her water all over your multi-million dollar contracts, or house deeds, or whatever it was you held," she later wrote in a column.[2] Immediately, Kate began rubbing the man's arm, probably because she liked the soft feel of his jacket. And throughout the flight, Kate called the stranger "Daddy," not because she confused him with her own father, but because he felt "safe" to her.

"You could have shifted uncomfortably in your seat," Shanell wrote. "You could have ignored her. You could have given me that 'smile' that I despise because it means; 'manage your child please.' You did none of that. You engaged Kate in conversation and you asked her questions about her turtles. She could never really answer your questions but she was so enamored with you that she kept eye contact and joint attention on the items you were asking her about. I watched and smiled. I made a few polite offers to distract her, but you would have none of it."

When Kate noticed the man's iPad, she said, "Is dis Daddy's puduter?" The man replied that, yes, it was his iPad, and offered to let her see it. The little girl thought he was offering it to her to keep, but her mom said, "Look with your eyes, Kate. That is not yours." To which Kate replied, "Dat's nice!"

The man then noticed Kate's own iPad and said, "I like your computer, too. It has a nice purple case." Not long afterwards, Kate asked the man, "Daddy wanna be a bad guy?" and offered him her Shredder doll—"and that, my friend," Shanell wrote, "is high praise."

And so it went throughout the flight. Toward the end of the trip, Kate had "reached her limit" and screamed, over and over, for her mom to open the jet's door and let her out of the "cwosed" (closed) plane. The man tried to distract Kate, to no avail; but his unsuccessful efforts still made this harried mom "emotional."

When Shanell finally sat down to write a moving tribute to the anonymous "Daddy in 16C," as she called him, she had one final thing to say:

> So, thank you. Thank you for not making me repeat
> those awful apologetic sentences that I so often say in pub-
> lic. Thank you for entertaining Kate so much that she had

---

2 Shanell Mouland, "Dear 'Daddy in Seat 16C." January 13, 2014. http://www.huffingtonpost.com/shanell-mouland/dear-daddy-in-seat-16c_b_4585865.html

her most successful plane ride, yet. And, thank you for putting your papers away and playing turtles with our girl.

Did this man's choice to interact with an autistic three-year-old cost him some valuable time that he had planned to spend with some important papers in his briefcase? Perhaps. Will the three of these strangers ever meet again? Probably not. But whether they ever reunite, I believe the brief interaction itself was worth the effort it took.

Even short interactions on The Coil can make someone's day a little brighter or reinforce a worthwhile connection. Connection doesn't come only through long conversations or deep and involved interactions. Every time we intentionally interact with somebody through our coil, the incident fosters or reinforces a connection. Some of those interactions yield lifetime memories. On The Coil, you can proactively choose to take one shot and score a *lot* more than one goal.

MORE A SIEVE THAN A WALL

You cannot watch your coil at work for very long without realizing that personal growth and business growth are inevitably related. We often like to think of them as totally separate entities, walled off from one another, like East from West or night from day. But in real life, that "wall" looks much more like a sieve, with personal elements continually oozing into the business sector, and vice versa.

A well-known grad school in Dallas once asked "Bill," one of my consults, to give a series of lectures at the institution. When he told me about the engagement, I asked, "Who do you know on campus?"

"Well, I know the president," Bill replied. "We went to school together."

"And have you called the president?" I asked.

"Well . . . no."

"But you were classmates," I continued. "Why don't you call him? You could say, 'I'm going to be on campus. Do you have time for coffee?'"

It simply hadn't occurred to Bill to proactively engage his coil. So I gently encouraged him to do just that: "You've just identified a potential relationship, a good contact. You have some downtime. So why don't you reach out?"

Here's a guy who knows lots of people and is very successful, but he hadn't considered the advantages of engaging his coil without some specific *professional* goal in mind. I wanted him to recognize and come to accept that The Coil functions on a far greater scope than mere vocation alone; usually we choose to engage it without some specific expectation in mind. And who knows what such efforts might later yield?

So Bill called the school president, who said, "Great to hear from you! It's been a long time. I'd *love* to see you! Come on by." The two men set up an appointment, had a wonderful conversation, and reinvigorated what had been a dormant contact. Bill's single decision to reach out has led to several other unexpected opportunities.

I should emphasize, though, that Bill didn't reach out *in order to* create some new opportunities for his business. He had no agenda in contacting the school president, other than to reconnect with an old school buddy. But if you reconnect with the president of a significant grad school in a large city like Dallas, and you really want to do more business and have more contacts in that metropolitan area, then guess who knows a bunch of other leaders within that community?

Your coil is a lot better at building bridges than constructing walls. It tends to be color blind and doesn't naturally distinguish between the "gold" of your business life and the "green" of your personal life— and most of the time, that turns out to be a very, very good thing.

A FIRM COMMITMENT TO ADD VALUE

Norm Sonju was my first boss out of college; he headed up the company's commercial services division. A few years after I joined the company, Norm left to become President and General Manager of the NBA's Dallas Mavericks. Just this week, I got a personal letter from him.

Now, I can't remember the last time Norm and I exchanged letters. But out of the blue, he coiled back. He wrote, he said, because he wondered if I'd had any contact with Dave, the guy who long ago had served as the head of finance for our old division. Norm knew that Dave and I had become good friends after my first knee surgery, just a couple of years out of college. It was 1972, I was single, I was hurting physically, and I had nowhere to go. Dave said to me, "Why don't you come with my wife and me and recover at our home?" I gladly accepted his generous offer. That experience led to a lifelong friendship. Since then, we've traveled around the world together, partnered on some business ventures, and have continued to stay in touch.

Norm also had done some business with Dave, but somewhere along the line, the two of them had lost touch. Norm had just had two knees replaced himself and told me he was sitting at home, thinking about old contacts and trying to figure out what might be next for him. Through his coil, he reached back to our relationship, and by doing so, set in motion the reconnection of three people.

That same day, by sheer coincidence, I received an email from Dave. I also had just gone through another knee surgery, and he wanted to hear about my recovery. I'll soon circle back with both men and get them directly reconnected. I don't know if I can be of any other assistance to them, but I'll find out.

This is The Coil at work. It's not merely about connecting and reconnecting, but also about proactively asking ourselves, "Am I adding value? Do I tend to leave people better off after our interactions than they were before? Would they consider our exchange worthwhile in some way, if even just to brighten their day a bit or prompt a smile?"

Not long ago, I introduced two friends whom I thought might enjoy getting connected. I'd known Larry, an M.D., for many years. He and I first met after I offered the use of my boat to take a visiting English dignitary on a bird watching trip to Catalina Island; Larry joined us as a board member of the man's organization. In the years since,

I've come to know Bill, who works in the ophthalmology industry. Since both men have an interest in nonprofit work in the Majority World, I guessed that they might find some areas of mutual interest.

They have. Through the Tropical Health Alliance Foundation, Larry and Bill have found some ways to work together to improve eye care in Ethiopia, where an estimated 860,000 men and women have gone blind from untreated cataracts. About 80 percent of Ethiopia's population lives on less than two dollars a day, and the country averages only one ophthalmologist per 1.25 million individuals. The U.S., by comparison, has one such specialist for every 17,300 individuals.

I recently received an email from Larry, thanking me for connecting him with Bill. That email concluded with five exclamation points, so I know Larry appreciates the tiny role I played in sparking this new partnership. What these two men already have accomplished in a neglected part of world reinforces for me the crucial importance of adding value through The Coil. It also reminds me that adding value usually doesn't take much effort; in fact, just making such a commitment makes it likely that value will get added.

PROACTIVELY BECOMING MORE SELF-AWARE

Just as your coil requires a certain amount of give and take, so it demands a heightened self-awareness. Fortunately, regularly engaging with your coil also has a strong tendency to help you *become* more self-aware.

For my fiftieth birthday party, I chartered John Wayne's former yacht. I hosted about 125 guests from nearly all walks of life. I really looked forward to seeing how the varied members of this eclectic group would interact with one another. I had friends who sported more tattoos than they did unmarked skin. I had mechanics, successful millionaire business people, pastors and ministry leaders. I had invited men and women, young people and the elderly.

I had a *great* time observing how such a wide assortment of humanity connected . . . or struggled to. It fascinated me. Many of my guests, perhaps even most, found it difficult to transition between groups. Every person there had received an invitation because I considered him or her a dear friend, and I wanted them all to know how I connected to each of them, despite their highly disparate backgrounds.

As I watched my guests interacting (or not), it struck me that the individuals who enjoyed the most success at "crossing barriers" seemed to be those who had a higher level of self-awareness. The key factor in determining who most effectively and enjoyably reached out across social boundaries was not, as I might have expected, the difference between extroverts and introverts. I saw introverted, conservative couples having great conversations with young, tattooed singles, and I also observed extroverted, energetic thirty-somethings mingling almost exclusively with their own "kind." Having an extroverted or introverted personality seemed to correlate more with the volume of connections made than with their breadth.

A strong sense of self-awareness tends to give us the confidence to leave our shells and explore the fascinating world of people and things around us. And every time we choose to shed our cocoons and reach out, our confidence only grows. It's a lot like building muscle. You gain strength through stretching and exercising your muscles, and the more you do so, the stronger you get. In a similar way, while it takes a certain amount of self-awareness to successfully engage with your coil, the more you do so, the more self-aware you become—and the more success you can achieve through the interactions it makes possible.

MAKE IT INTO A GAME

If you want to keep some genuine excitement in your life, consciously employ your coil in play mode. Make it into a game. Enjoy it. Experiment with it. See how it might function in totally random environments. I do this myself and I encourage my clients and associates to do the same.

I received an email the other day from a friend who recently decided to give this strategy a try. While I doubt that everyone would feel as comfortable as he did with his experiment, I still think it provides an excellent illustration of the play possibilities of your coil:

When I flew into Oakland last week, my flight was an hour delayed. That hour delay meant that I missed the last BART train back to San Francisco, and I was either 1) stuck in Oakland for the night, or 2) stuck paying for a cab back to the city.

I figured I was not the only one in this boat, so I pulled out my iPad and scribbled, "Anyone want to split a cab to SF?" I raised it above my head. Within five seconds, I kid you not, a short Indian guy walked up to me. He worked for Google and had just returned from three months abroad. He'd moved to the Bay only a couple months before that. He was taking a cab back to the city. His name was Sam.

Two days later, Sam and I ended up going rock climbing together—he'd forgotten his jacket in the cab and I'd found it when I got to my place, which conveniently forced us to actually make the vague "we should hang out sometime" a reality.

Tonight, he and a bunch of his acquaintances went out to dinner, and he invited me. I sat next to Gabe, who is opening up a bar/nightclub downtown, and Colleen, who works for a random startup and grew up in Hong Kong but went to University of Kentucky (in fact, I just met a coworker of hers in my online dating adventures), and any number of other interesting people (don't really need to list them all here).

We ate. We talked. I shared a bunch of stories, from whitewater rafting to online dating, and was generally the catalyst for a party of a bunch of people who barely knew one another.

Not much of a story beyond that, but I'm reminded that likely I'll run into some of these people in a year or two.

I love the way my young friend ended his email. It reveals that he clearly understands both *what* he's doing and *why*. "The Coil will get ever bigger," he wrote, "for those willing to take a risk."

To get the most out of your coil—and equally, to most effectively give to others through it—takes intentionality. It requires a proactive approach. So recognize its power, but also consciously choose to engage with it. Even in the most unlikely of places.

CHAPTER 5

Unconscious Doesn't Mean Unthinking

L ately I've been spending increasing amounts of time with a local research university and some of the wonderful people in its graduate division. There's no obvious reason why I should be doing this, leading discussions on business and leadership issues. The story, though, illustrates how putting your coil habitually to work significantly increases your connections and enriches your experience of life.

My wife is an artist who several years ago wanted to learn a new style of painting. So Antje went to the local junior college and there met another artist who had recently retired as the associate Chancellor at the university. The two became friends and introduced their husbands to each other.

Sometime later, the university decided to honor Antje's friend and we were asked if we would like to attend the event. To support our friend, we said yes. Since we didn't know anyone there, it surprised us to receive a call asking if we had any seating preferences. "No," we replied, "we're coming only to honor our friend."

We received a second surprise when we arrived at the event and found our table and seat assignments very near the front. As we sat down, my wife whispered in my ear, "Although we may not know the people sitting next to us, their names and pictures are in the program." I looked, and it turned out that the dean of the university's graduate division had been seated right next to me.

The two of us had a delightful conversation and began to see that we had a number of ideas in sync with one another, especially regarding the academy. By evening's end, she asked if I might be willing to speak at a graduate division function. I agreed, and since then have spent a considerable amount of time interacting with students and faculty. I have thoroughly enjoyed all of it.

But why did it happen at all?

It happened because Antje and I chose several years ago to make The Coil a regular part of our lifestyle. As a result, we get to enjoy a stream of interesting connections that often usher us into fascinating parts of the world that, otherwise, would have remained totally unknown to us. Through that single art school class, for example, a whole new realm of opportunities and experiences has opened up for us.

Your coil works best for you when you make it a part of your daily lifestyle. When you engage with it regularly, as a habit—something you naturally do because you enjoy it and not as something you have to do to get ahead—surprising things often result. As you keep your antenna up, ask appropriate questions, and remain inquisitive about the world and the people around you, making new connections becomes the norm.

At this stage of my life, engaging with my own coil has become almost an unconscious process. I don't think, *Oh, here would be a perfect opportunity to engage The Coil.* I just automatically start listening, observing, asking questions, and trying to see what interesting connections might result. It's not a forced activity for me, but a very natural one. It's fun. I like it. And very often, it leads to things far beyond mere fun.

ONE STEP AT A TIME

I'm not selling a magic potion here, nor am I advocating a highly prescriptive approach like *Seven Super Steps to Stupendous Security and Success!* Making your coil a habit, a lifestyle choice, is a one-step-at-a-time process. It's bound to feel somewhat unnatural and a little uncomfortable at first, just as it feels to most children when they first start learning how to ride a bike. But the more you choose to engage with your coil, the more natural and comfortable it feels, and the more productive the process becomes.

When Antje and I first met, The Coil didn't yet have much of a place in her life. She typically didn't engage with it, certainly not on a regular basis. The more time we spent together, however, the more aware of it she became, because it is a part of who I am. As she began to both see and recognize the benefits that frequently came to us, the more she wanted to put her coil's power to work. Today, it's just as much a part of her as it is of me.

Are there days when I don't want to engage with my coil? Certainly. Sometimes, you just want to be a wallflower. On days like that, it feels *good* to be a wallflower, and there's nothing wrong or odd about that. I remember what Tony Campolo said about this many years ago. Tony is a high-voltage speaker, author, and professor of sociology at Eastern College in Philadelphia. He also speaks often at churches and for various special events. He said that when he finishes some speaking engagement and gets on the plane to go home, usually he feels full of energy and stimulated by the event he just left. So when someone sitting next to him asks, "What do you do for a living?" he tells them he's a sociologist, and off zooms the conversation. Sometimes, though, he feels drained and doesn't feel like talking. At those times, when his exhaustion has him dragging and the passenger next to him asks, "What do you do for a living?" Tony replies, quite truthfully, "I'm a Baptist evangelist." End of conversation.

Normally, though, habitually engaging with The Coil adds a richness to life that I would not willingly give up. Hardly a day goes by that I don't have some kind of "coil story." And so my friends and associates are likely to hear me say, "there it goes again!"

SOMETIMES THE COIL HAS GREAT BUSINESS SIGNIFICANCE . . .

Many of my current and most important business connections came to me through my coil. Through it, for example, I first got connected to author Dr. Henry Cloud, which has led to many other significant connections.

In the beginning, I didn't know Henry Cloud from Adam. I had never read any of his excellent books. But one day I got a call from Scott Bolinder, who then served as executive publisher for a Grand Rapids publishing house. I'd known of Scott since college, although he was a few years younger than I. Over the years, the two of us had stayed in touch, at least a little. He knew that I liked boats. Scott called and said, "I have an author who likes boats as much as you do. He could use a financial partner on it."

"Great to hear from you, Scott," I said. "I'm glad you have an author who likes boats, but I already have a nice boat that I bought just six months ago. I'm not looking for another boat. And I'm particularly not looking for somebody who needs a financial partner on his boat."

Scott continued regardless. "His name is Henry Cloud," he said.

"Okay, great," I replied. "Tell me about Henry Cloud."

"Well, he's a psychologist. And he's written a lot of books on relationships and boundaries and personal growth, things like that. I'd love it if at least you could meet him. He lives in your area."

"I'll tell you what," I answered, "I'll ask my wife."

When I told her of my conversation with Scott, I found out immediately that she *had* read a lot of Henry's books. "Oh, at least go meet him," she said, with a good deal of enthusiasm. "I really like his ideas."

So I called Scott and relayed my wife's strong endorsement. He encouraged me to call Henry, which I did. But I doubted much would come of it.

My doubts vanished, just a few minutes into our initial meeting. We had a great conversation about leadership and about a number of other things. We hit it off so well that we soon got in business together, which led to many other good things. Many of the ideas we discussed even made it into a few of his books.

Just last week, after my knee surgery, I got a note from Henry. "Greg," he said, "I hope you are well. How is the knee? I want to hear your story." He continued, "I got some good news today about *Boundaries for Leaders* [a 2013 book] that I wanted to share with you. It's been nominated as one of eight finalists for leadership book of the year."

I wrote back and told Henry I had a lot of fun reading that book, in part because I recognized a few of our stories from several years before. I told him I felt very grateful for the legacy that had come out of our interaction—a classic coil story.

That isn't where my coil connections ended in the story, of course. It was through Henry that I met John Townsend, his partner and co-author, with whom I've probably spent even more hours than I have with Henry. And John, in turn, has introduced me to many other individuals and opportunities. One of Henry's other connections, Tony, used to serve with me on the board of the Los Angeles Mission. We became good friends through our service there.

One day Tony called and said, "Greg, I wonder if you would come down and talk to my wife about her business? We think we could use some good counsel." I thought, *This is interesting. Here's one of the smartest business guys I've ever met, asking me to come down and talk to his wife about her business.*

But I said, "sure." And so over the next few weeks, we spent some significant time together, mostly having fun. Later that year, the family invited me to Thanksgiving at their home. What a story they have! I had a great time with them that holiday season and came away with a memory I'll always cherish.

This is how The Coil often works, especially when we make it a part of our daily lives. There's no telling where it may lead or where it may go. The coil story I just told began with Scott Bolinder, who knows nothing about Tony. And yet Scott was the primary agent who got me, over time, to a meeting and eventually a friendship with Tony. The Coil is great at this kind of thing. And when we make it a natural part of the way we live, things like it are far more likely to occur.

. . . AND SOMETIMES IT DOESN'T

When you engage with your coil as part of your regular routine, you increasingly value new connections just for the sake of those connections, whether they "go someplace" or not. Consider what frequently happens when you board an airplane.

Some people want to talk. Others don't. When someone puts on a headset, sits back and closes his eyes, he's obviously saying, "While I'm sure you're a perfectly fascinating person, I would much rather you didn't bother me." But most often, probably, your seat mates are not only open for a conversation, but interested in one.

Or, maybe they just forgot their headset.

On a trip I took just last week, I sat by three different people on the four legs of my flight. With every one of them, I had at least a minimal conversation. And in each case, I found some place to connect.

The first person wondered about my surgically repaired knee. Would the long flight to Europe be a problem for me? We never discussed business; in fact, I have no idea what she does for a living.

The second individual works in real estate, especially with retail shopping. He came alive when I mentioned the name of a prominent realty company. I described a little of what I'd done in the past and then asked a lot of questions. I haven't done retail for a quarter of a century, but I knew enough and remembered enough to say, "I know a little of the stuff you're running into, at least historically. I wonder how it's changed?" When I turned the conversation to him, he delighted to let me know.

By the end of that leg of my trip, he gave me his card. It surprised me a bit, because we hadn't had that kind of a conversation. We never said, "let's stay in touch." But I knew what he was saying: "I want you to remember me." The connection, although brief, meant something to him, and to me. And that "something" had very little to do with business and nothing to do with working together.

My last passenger buddy worked as a developer. He described to me the many zoning problems he had with a particular tract of housing.

"That's interesting, your work on that project," I said. "I've just joined the advisory board of a real estate company in that area. It started in the gravel business out in Riverside County, and now it's doing all kinds of industrial work in the area."

"Oh, I've seen their signs," he replied. And once again, two strangers found a common language. In all three cases, I listened and observed and asked enough questions to try to find something that could drive us to a different level of relationship. Why? For the sheer possibility of learning something new.

That's the challenge of engaging with your coil, when you do so as a lifestyle. Did any of those brief plane conversations radically change my life? Did they give me a new purpose on this earth? Did I find some great new business opportunity through any of them? Hardly. But again, that's not the point. I did learn some new things and I have reason to believe I managed to affirm at least one person (the unexpected business card tells me that). At other times and on other planes, I've been the one affirmed. You can't dictate what your coil will bring to you. But you can choose, every day, whether you will even give it the chance.

MENTORING YOUNG LEADERS

Our culture loves to throw around buzzwords. One such current term is "mentor." Businesses use it, churches use it, academic institutions use it, and so do many other organizations and groups. I hope the term doesn't become just the next cliché-du-jour, however, because our society needs seasoned mentors.

I have reached a stage in life where I'd like to think I have accumulated enough depth of experience to enter into a few helpful mentoring relationships. With that in mind, I have chosen to spend part of my time consulting and mentoring young leaders. Most of the young leaders I mentor came to me through my coil.

Several years ago, I consulted with a former pro athlete who wanted some counsel on running a tax exempt service organization. A few years after that, the same man asked if I would help mentor his son, "Jim." I did so periodically at various stages of Jim's career, but not regularly.

And then one day, Jim got a job helping to manage a small manufacturing business. Once that happened, I said, "If we're going to continue doing this, you'll have to actually start paying me." His company accepted the proposal, I met with the owner, and together we worked out what we wanted to accomplish. About two months into the arrangement, Jim told me, "Greg, this has been really, really helpful. I've met some other guys here who have a different business. Would you be willing to talk to them?"

I agreed and soon met his friends, a couple of thirty-somethings who together had started an Internet technology business. As a mentor and consultant, I got very involved in both their business and their lives, because it's never just the business. One of them had gone through a divorce and was struggling with its fallout, including his strained relationship with his son. The other had some serious "family of origin" issues that significantly affected his ability to run his business. Over time, we saw growth in both their business and their personal lives.

Eventually the pair said to me, "This has really been helpful, Greg. Now, we have a young guy who does our insurance. Would you be willing to talk to him?"

Again, I said, "sure." The two of us started talking, and in the year since, his business has quadrupled. The growth has allowed him to move from his parents' tiny building to a much larger place of his own. He's gone from a staff of one to a staff of four. It's still a very small business, but that small company has gone through a radical change that has required him to walk through some significant issues with his parents and other close relatives. So the mentoring hasn't been merely about building a business; it's been about how to build character, knowing who you are, and remembering where you came from.

In every one of these cases—from father, to son, to friends, to business associate—the respective businesses have enjoyed significant growth. But just as importantly, in every case there's also been *personal* growth. How could it be otherwise? The two are almost never unrelated. Good mentoring, which I hope I've provided, understands that principle and acts on it.

I've told you this "coil story" because it embodies so much of what The Coil is and does. In none of those circumstances did I raise a flag and go out to market myself, as if to say, "Hey, I'm available. Call me." One relationship naturally led to another relationship, which led to a third, and then a fourth. That's how most of my "business" comes to me, through my coil.

The Coil goes where it wills, and it has such a strong indifference to the idea of a separation between business life and personal life that I could nearly call it contempt. If you go to your coil *only* for business growth, then you likely will have more than a few, shall we say, missteps. If you go to your coil *only* for personal growth, then likely you will find there a good deal more than you bargained for. But if you go to your coil regularly, habitually, as a lifestyle, looking forward to whatever it may wash up on your shore on any given day, then you are very likely to find pieces of real delight.

A LIFE WITHOUT PRESCRIPTIONS

I admit it: I have never liked a prescriptive approach to life. In most cases, life is much too complicated for *Seven Keys to X or The Ten Secrets of Y.* And yet, publishers know that "seven keys" and "ten secrets" do, at least, have some power to sell books.

(I just looked up on Amazon book titles that include the two phrases just mentioned. The first came back with 15,392 hits, the second with 5,422. That's a lot of secrets, and even more keys! I wonder where one might keep them all?)

If you *really* want seven keys to The Coil or ten secrets of your coil, I am afraid you will have to find another book. While I could whip up some kind of prescription, I doubt very much it would be much more than a placebo. And it might fester into a poison.

So in place of a prescription, let me repeat what I've already said. The Coil works best when you engage it as a matter of habit. When in your normal routine, day in and day out, you tap into the power of your coil, then you are most likely to see it work its surprising "magic." As it becomes a part of who you are and enters the warp and woof of your daily existence, your coil will enrich your life with a steady stream of . . . *who knows?*

CHAPTER 6

At the End of the Day, It's All Chocolate

don't normally notice them except at Christmas. You've probably seen versions of them, those generic-looking brown paper bags imprinted with words like "GRAB BAG." Sellers entice you to buy one for some nominal fee, the catch being that you won't know the contents of the bag until you go home and open it. Very often, the seller "guarantees" that each bag contains merchandise worth at least such and such . . . but also that a few of the nondescript bags hide treasures worth far more than the selling price. Could you be one of the lucky ones to hit the jackpot? Well, why not buy one and try your luck? The worst that can happen is that you (or the person to whom you give the bag) become the new owner of some memorable little trinket; and in any case, you've had the fun of the chase.

The Coil works a lot like that. In exchange for the little it costs you to engage with it, it promises to bless you with some benefit of undisclosed size and shape. You never know what The Coil might bring you, whether something small and fun or something huge and critically important.

But the only way to get anything at all from The Coil is to give it a try.

The life motto of the classic film character Forrest Gump fits really well here. Your coil, too, is "like a box of chocolates. You never know what you're gonna get." As we've seen, the benefits may be practical, informative, or just fun. They might be important, interesting, or merely for enjoyment. But each of those benefits is worthy in their own right. They're all chocolates, just different tasty varieties.

A CROP OF ASSORTED REWARDS

Although The Coil is all about relationships, it's also about growing in all areas of life. When you engage with The Coil as a lifestyle, therefore, you should expect to see some rewards in multiple dimensions of your life.

One day, you might gain some frivolous knowledge. On another day, you might encourage someone who really needs it. I once got asked, for example, to review a manuscript written by a scientist from the Jet Propulsion Laboratory, an expert in quantum mechanics. I don't believe I understood half of what he wrote, but since it seemed to me that he'd written three books rather than one, I encouraged him to focus on just one of them. Through that encounter, I learned some things I never would have otherwise, and I got to encourage a new friend.

Through your coil, you might meet someone who challenges you to be a better person. Another person might encourage you to go in a different direction, professionally or personally. And almost certainly, you'll find someone on your coil who can help you at a critical juncture to achieve more than you could on your own.

I know I'm mixing metaphors here, but for a moment, picture your coil as a huge farm where you grow an enormous variety of crops. From corn to rutabegas, from spinach to watermelons, your farm generates a staggering variety of produce—but all of it is food. Some of it you eat, some of it others eat. In certain seasons you harvest more vegetables, and in other seasons you get more fruit. As you carefully and persistently cultivate your fields, your farm grows and yields larger and larger harvests.

The variety of "crops" produced by The Coil fascinates me. I love it all. Sometimes it helps me expand my business. Sometimes it's pure fun. Sometimes it allows me to help somebody else. In all cases, it enables me to improve myself, not necessarily in the sense of generating a huge financial boon, but in making me a better *me*.

Think of your coil, in other words, as a multidimensional approach to personal growth. That's one of the main ways we've seen how it differs from networking, which usually focuses on business alone. When we have just one thing on our mind, pretty much nothing else matters. If we focus only on corn, then all the wheat and apples and onions and grapes and lettuce popping up all around us will likely wither and die without ever gracing our table.

Since I like variety, I have chosen to adopt the multidimensional approach. I enjoy this "who knows what's coming next" aspect of The Coil. I like not knowing where it'll take me. I love the idea that I'm going to get something interesting, whether it be this, or that, or something else again. A one-dimensional approach lacks the power to give me that kind of diversity. And so I engage with my coil, not only because I need something, but because it's a good thing to do. Period.

A BLAST FROM THE PAST

I attended high school my junior and senior years in a little southwest Minnesota town. My older brother had left a university in South Carolina to attend another school in South Dakota, and at that time his girlfriend moved to our town. The pair had decided to get married, but couldn't do so until he graduated. She began looking for a job and eventually found one as a live-in nanny with the wealthiest family in the area. She took care of their kids and traveled throughout the United States with them, and at least once to Mexico. As a result, she developed a very tight bond with the children.

Every time I visit my brother and sister-in-law, a special painting hanging in their home prompts me to recall this story. It's the only original oil painting in their whole house, given to them on their wedding day by this wealthy Minnesota family.

I'd heard a lot about this wonderful family through the years, but I had never met any of its members. So far as I knew, they all still lived in Minnesota, while I have lived for years in Southern California.

One of my consults, "Ted," met a member of this family through a coil unrelated to mine. This man and his wife had been looking for some estate counsel and someone advised them to contact Ted. Shortly thereafter, Ted decided to throw a Christmas party that would include a few prospective clients, in addition to a large group of friends and acquaintances. This couple made the list. When Ted showed me his roll of invitees, I scanned it and said, "I know that family name. Let me check to see if, by some coincidence, it's the same family from my home town." I called my sister-in-law, even though I saw no benefit for me personally. On the off chance it could help Ted, however, I made the call.

"Do you know a man by this name?" I asked her.

"Oh, yeah," she replied. "He was the littlest of the kids I took care of. He was in diapers when I first went there and was a toddler by the time I left." Since her marriage, she said, she hadn't had much contact with the family, a period of several decades.

"Okay," I said, "thanks. That's good to know."

Before then, I knew that Ted's contact worked in the same industry as the Minnesota family. So by the time I hung up the phone, I knew that Ted's prospective client and the person my sister-in-law had taken care of so many years before were very likely the same individual. Not many people share the same unusual last name and the same unique business.

When I next saw Ted, I told him, "Make sure you introduce me to this guy, because I want to meet him."

The day of the party, though, Ted got so busy with all of his guests that he forgot to make the introduction. I'd undergone leg surgery not long before the party, and when my leg started bothering me, I told him, "I think we need to go. But you still haven't introduced me to the couple."

"Oh, okay," he replied, "I'll go get them."

In a few moments, the husband and wife came by and we started to talk. Very quickly, I knew The Coil had done it again. "Do you remember my sister-in-law, Mary?" I asked.

Without saying a word, he reached into his pocket and pulled out his iPhone. He fiddled with it and brought up an old photo that looked to be from about 1967. I found myself staring at a long-ago picture of my brother and sister-in-law, standing in this family's house around Christmas time. After all those years, this man still carried that picture with him.

And then the real fun began.

"I liked Mary a lot," he said. "But I didn't like your brother."

"Really? Why not?"

"Well, he took my Mary away from me," he said, grinning.

Clearly, he still cherished a great memory of his nanny, my sister-in-law. So if nothing more than that happened on this night, it would have been worth it. I would have helped him reconnect to a wonderful, sentimental memory. But because Antje also has become a devoted user of The Coil, she noticed something in our conversation and asked a somewhat off-the-wall question of the man's wife. They started a new discussion and The Coil went to work once more.

It turned out that both women are of German descent. They immediately began speaking in German and quickly bonded at another level. They discovered that each of their fathers had emigrated from the same area in what used to be East Germany, just over the Polish border.

By the time we left the party, I was able both to affirm this couple and to affirm Ted's credentials as a professional. And in that unexpected way, this couple—who had driven an hour and a half to the party without knowing anyone there—could feel good both about their choice to attend and about the possibility of retaining Ted. The Coil had reached all the way back to my childhood to do its thing.

None of this would have happened if I had ignored or dismissed the name on Ted's party list. But since The Coil is all about relationship, I allowed my curiosity to prompt me to call my sister-in-law. I didn't have to make the call. I could have approached the man cold and said, "Hi, I'm Greg Campbell. You should use Ted." But such an endorsement would have had far less of an impact than it did after we talked about his former nanny. Our little chat put him in an entirely different mood, so that when we talked briefly about Ted, I became something other than just a shill for my friend. The two of us had lived in the same town. I was connected by marriage to his beloved nanny. So when I followed through on my commitment to Ted to affirm his professional qualifications, my words carried a very different kind of weight than they would have had I not bothered to tap into the surprising power of The Coil.

VALUE THE EXPERIENCE ITSELF

I set out in this chapter to describe the many benefits of The Coil. But in the end, its greatest benefit may be the experience itself. Yes, your coil can spark warm memories, help forge new business relationships, and allow you to bless others, along with a thousand other things. But I have grown to value most the experience itself. I look forward to the surprising new things it lays at my feet, often in the most unexpected of ways. And that new thing may have no pragmatic component to it at all. *That was nice,* I think after watching my coil perform some little bit of unanticipated magic.

It's all chocolate.

I love it when that chocolate comes rich and gigantic and bursting with delicious flavor; but to be frank, I wouldn't want a steady diet of that. Over the years, I have learned to love, in a very different way, those times when my coil offers me a small, mild, delicate piece of chocolate that disappears almost before I pop it into my mouth. That's what keeps me coming back for more.

TAKE OFF THE PRESSURE

When you consciously curb your expectations of what your coil may send your way, you reduce a lot of the pressure. It naturally becomes more fun, because you don't have to think, *Oh, I could be wasting my time here.* If you remain content to receive a small chocolate rather than a titanic one, how could you be "wasting" your time?

Some of my friends struggle a bit here, especially those of us who take our religious faith seriously. While I'm all for a robust faith, some of us have a tendency to turn it into something moist and sticky, something that too often gums up the works and stops the gears from turning. We tend to approach too many things in life with a deadly serious, more-earnest-than-death expectation of some supernatural, divine encounter. We see an unexpected name pop up on an email and instantly think, *Wow, what is God trying to do here?* We bump into the friend of a friend of a friend of a semi-famous business guru and think, *Here we go, it's like Pharaoh elevating Joseph to Prime Minister of Egypt!*

While I believe that God is in every part of life—and I'm overwhelmingly grateful for that reality—I have no reason to believe that he fills anyone's life with a steady stream of Red Sea crossings, enabling them every hour to cross over to the Promised Land on a seabed made repeatedly dry. Life is full of mundane moments and pedestrian periods, and we must not expect that every coil encounter should have some deeper meaning designed to shake the pillars of the universe. While I believe a robust faith can indeed influence what comes to us through our coils, I think that same faith should better equip us to relax and receive with an open hand whatever comes our way, whether it's little stuff or big stuff.

Forgive me, but sometimes a pipe is just a pipe.

Beware of turning your coil into something deadly serious. While I believe in "divine appointments," not every coil encounter produces a hush in heaven. Continually looking for deep significance in every happenstance can torpedo the fun that your coil has the capacity to deliver. You don't need that kind of disappointment, and neither do I.

So if the Good Lord has freely given us all things to enjoy, as we're told, then by all means, let's enjoy what he gives. Let's not lose that enjoyment by imagining that a fun little encounter is really a platinum key to the universe, or a delicious lemon truffle might be, in fact, the deed to Willy Wonka's whole empire. Let's tone down the expectations. Let's take off the pressure. And let's enjoy the ride.

GUARD YOUR EXPECTATIONS

So where does all of this go? Who knows? That's the adventure of your coil. The best advice I can give you is this: *Follow the current and see where it takes you.*

Learn to relish the adventure, enjoy the journey, and exult in the discovery, whatever its size or shape. Guard your expectations; don't let them shrink to a single variety or class of desired benefits. We ask these questions and pursue these clues even when we have no reason to believe there's anything in it for us. We don't look for a life-changing relationship from every person who joins our coil. A new connection may not bring even a hint of promise for personal financial gain.

But what is intrigue "worth"? What dollar value can we place on exhilaration or fascination? When a new connection broadens our horizons in a way we never imagined, how can we know what that gift will do for us in the future? And so we pursue the intriguing simply because it intrigues us.

Although I occasionally describe the "magic" that often results when you engage with The Coil, you know as well as I do that its power has nothing to do with magic. There is no 1-2-3 step process that will deliver to your doorstep everything you want, no mystical incantation that will make some cherished dream come true. At times, The Coil can indeed seem like Aladdin's Cave of Wonders; but no genie exists to make those wonders appear at your command. You can wish all you want, but realize that your coil is nearly deaf to specific requests. It does what it does.

But remember, it's all chocolate.

SUCCESSFUL LEADERS COIL

The most successful leaders I know all have inquiring minds and make room for their inquisitive natures to express themselves. Many of them even like to think of themselves as philosophers. Certainly, they maintain a lively curiosity about how things work and how they might be able to work even better.

The leaders I know who have a desire to "get to the top" are constantly searching for more knowledge about their job, their organization, and their industry. But while they know how to focus, they also know the value of letting their curiosity run a bit, allowing it to explore uncharted territories.

Almost always, once they understand what The Coil is and does, they universally take steps to making it a part of their regular routines. Even though it may take them a while to value a little thing as much as a gargantuan thing—to appreciate a peanut cluster as much as a chocolate cream pie—they come to see how their coil enriches their lives in a thousand ways. And most of the time, their employees take happy notice.

The late cartoonist Charles M. Schulz made a lot of people happy over the course of his long career, and I remember something he said that brought smiles to a lot of faces. "All you need is love," he declared. "But a little chocolate now and then doesn't hurt."

No, it doesn't. And since your coil happens to be a lot like a box of chocolates, you're the wiser if you dip into it whenever you get the chance.

A New Story Every Day

just received an unexpected email through an old AOL account that
I don't even use anymore. It just sort of popped up on my screen. *I
wonder what that is,* I thought as I worked on final touches for this
book. It came from an acquaintance I'll call Terry Smith.

It's a coil story.

I met Terry years ago in Southern California when he worked as a
finance guy for a big real estate company in downtown L.A. We connected at some event I can't even recall. Some months after that, I got
a call from him out of the blue, reintroducing himself.

"Greg," he said, "I've found out that [let's call it] Distinguished
University is hiring a guy, and I know you have a connection to the
school. I'm just wondering if I could talk to you about this position,
because I'm thinking of applying for it."

"That's really interesting," I replied. "Sure, tell me some more."

After we chatted for a few minutes, he told me he planned to visit
the school for some interviews with its board and president. "Tell me
who you're interviewing with," I said, "and I'll give you some background on all the people involved, so you can better prepare."

A few days later, he left for his visit. He called me after he returned and said, "I think it went pretty well, but I don't know for sure." We debriefed for a few minutes and then hung up.

A few minutes later, the school's president called me. "Greg," he said, "we've been interviewing this guy named Terry Smith."

"Yeah," I responded, "I know."

"Let me give you my assessment," he continued. "What do you think?"

I told him that I thought Terry would be a good hire for several reasons, which I listed. We talked a bit more, and by the end of our conversation, I had a strong sense that they planned to offer Terry the job.

Once I got off the phone with the president, I immediately called Terry. "Hey," I said, "I just finished talking to the university. I'm pretty sure the president is going to make you an offer. So you might want to start thinking about your response and what else you want to discuss with the school."

Within four hours, Terry got that call. He also got the job.

Because of a relationship I'd developed with Terry many years before, I had the privilege of helping him land a great position. I coached him when he contacted me from out of nowhere. I gave the university president some counsel. But I didn't leave it at that. I then chose proactively to go back to Terry and say, "Here's what I'm hearing. You might want to start thinking about your response and any other issues you believe you need to discuss."

Like many little tales, this one has a moral: *If you start regularly engaging with your coil, virtually every day you'll get a new story.*

I can't tell you the last time I heard from Terry; it's been several years. But the email I received from him today says he's coming to California. He wants to know if we can get together. What new story will come out of that reconnection? Again, who knows?

But that's what I like most about fresh stories. You get a different ending every day.